ROCKS, MINERALS, AND RESOURCES

Salt

John Paul Zronik

Crabtree Publishing Company
www.crabtreebooks.com

Crabtree Publishing Company

www.crabtreebooks.com

PMB 16A, 350 Fifth Avenue,
Suite 3308,
New York, NY 10118

612 Welland Avenue,
St. Catharines,
Ontario, Canada
L2M 5V6

73 Lime Walk,
Headington,
Oxford 0X3 7AD
United Kingdom

Coordinating editor: Ellen Rodger

Project editor: Carrie Gleason

Production coordinator: Rosie Gowsell

Designers: Brad Colotelo, Rosie Gowsell

Proofreader and Indexer: Wendy Scavuzzo

Production assistant: Samara Parent

Scanning technician: Arlene Arch-Wilson

Art director: Rob MacGregor

Photo research: Allison Napier

Prepress and printing: Worzalla Publishing Company

Consultants: Dr. Richard Cheel, Earth Sciences Department, Brock University

Project development: Focus Strategic Communication Inc.

Contributors: Rond Edwards, Jenna Dunlop

Photographs: AP/Wide World Photos: p. 12 (bottom), p. 14, p. 25 (bottom); Archivo Iconografico, S.A./CORBIS/MAGMA: p. 19 (top); John William Banagan: title page, p. 16 (top); Bettmann/CORBIS/ MAGMA: p. 15 (top), p. 20 (top), p. 25 (top); Richard Bickel/ CORBIS/MAGMA: p. 20 (bottom); MARTIN BOND/SCIENCE PHOTO LIBRARY: p. 9 (top); Craig J. Brown: p. 10 (bottom); MARTYN F. CHILLMAID/SCIENCE PHOTO LIBRARY: p. 27 (middle); Philip Coblentz: p. 23 (bottom); Anthony Cooper; Ecoscene/CORBIS/MAGMA: p. 17 (top); Bruce Dale: p. 6; Philippe Eranian/CORBIS/MAGMA: p.12 (top); Owen Franken/ CORBIS/MAGMA: p. 24 (top); Michael P. Gadomski/Photo Researchers, Inc.: p. 27 (bottom); Lowell Georgia/CORBIS/

MAGMA: p. 31 (bottom); PASCAL GOETGHELUCK/SCIENCE PHOTO LIBRARY: p. 23 (top); JAMES HOLMES, HAYS CHEMICALS/SCIENCE PHOTO LIBRARY: p. 27 (top, right); Jeremy Horner: p. 18; Mark Joseph: p. 31 (top); JAMES KING-HOLMES/SCIENCE PHOTO LIBRARY: p. 7 (bottom); MEHAU KULYK/SCIENCE PHOTO LIBRARY: p. 28 (right); ANDREW LAMBERT PHOTOGRAPHY/SCIENCE PHOTO LIBRARY: p. 26 (middle, right); George D. Lepp/CORBIS/MAGMA: p. 10 (top); Maximilian Stock Ltd/ Science Photo Library: p. 24 (bottom); Eric Meola: p. 7 (middle); DAVID PARKER/SCIENCE PHOTO LIBRARY: p. 22; JOE PASIEKA/SCIENCE PHOTO LIBRARY: p. 15 (bottom); LEA PATERSON/SCIENCE PHOTO LIBRARY: p. 29 (bottom); James Randklev/CORBIS/MAGMA: p. 8 (bottom); Carmen Redondo/CORBIS/MAGMA: p. 21 (bottom); Ricki Rosen/CORBIS SABA/MAGMA: p. 11 (top); ALEXIS ROSENFELD/SCIENCE PHOTO LIBRARY: p. 19 (bottom); Royalty-Free/CORBIS/MAGMA: p. 13; Kevin Schafer/CORBIS/ MAGMA: p. 17 (bottom); Blair Seitz/Photo Researchers Inc.: p. 29 (top); Janez Skok/CORBIS/MAGMA: cover; Staffan Widstrand/CORBIS/MAGMA: p. 16 (bottom); Other images from stock photo CD

Illustrations: Katherine Kantor: contents page, pp 4-5; Dan Pressman: p. 9, p. 11; Rob MacGregor: p.13

Cover: A salt worker carries a basket of salt from the Sambhar Salt Lakes, in eastern India.

Title page: These women are harvesting salt from seawater.

Cataloging-in-Publication Data

Zronik, John Paul, 1972
    Salt / John Paul Zronik.
       p. cm. -- (Rocks, minerals, and resources)
    Includes index.
    ISBN 0-7787-1411-X (rlb) -- ISBN 0-7787-1443-8 (pbk.)
  1. Salt--Juvenile literature.   I. Title. II.Series.
TN900.Z76 2004
553.6'32--dc22
                                        2004000819
                                              LC

Published by
Crabtree Publishing Company

Copyright © 2004

Contents

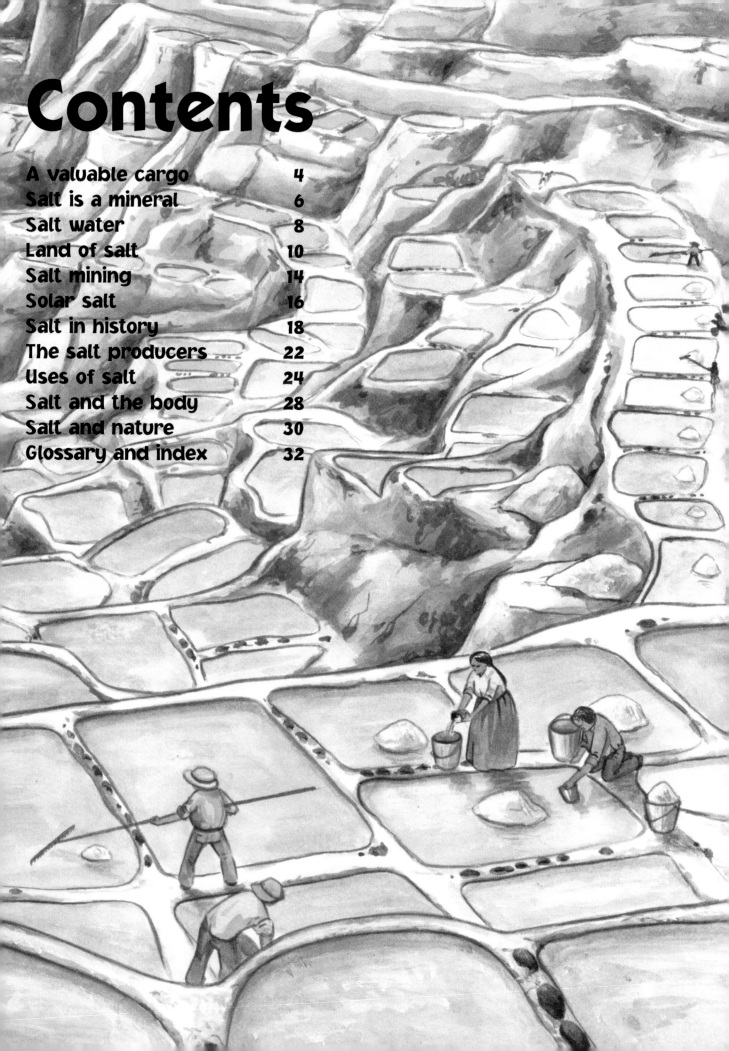

A valuable cargo

Across the dry Sahara desert, in north Africa, the Tuareg people use camel caravans to transport blocks of salt from mines in Taoudenni, 450 miles (724 kilometers) south to markets in Timbuktu. At the mines, merely 26 feet (8 meters) below the surface, 80-pound (36-kilogram) blocks of salt are cut from the Earth and carried to the surface, where they are stacked in wait for the journey. For over 2,000 years, the Sahara Salt Route, an unmarked desert road, has allowed people to earn a living by selling salt.

Salt - so common

At one time, salt was a rare and valued commodity. One thousand years ago, the Tuareg's caravans were as many as 40,000 camels long. Today, only 30 or 40 camels make up a caravan. Salt has now been discovered buried beneath the ground in almost every country in the world. It is one of the most common substances on Earth. In fact, there is such a large supply of salt in the oceans and buried underground, that it will probably never run out.

Salt is a mineral

Salt is used in a salt shaker as table salt or as rock salt on winter roads. It comes from the mineral halite. The word halite comes from the Greek word "hals", meaning salt.

Crystal cubes

Minerals are **chemical** substances that are found in the Earth and in the oceans. All minerals are crystals, which means their **atoms** are arranged in a regular **three-dimensional** repeating pattern. When minerals are broken, they always form a specific crystal shape. Halite forms cube-shaped crystals. The tiny grains of salt in a salt shaker are actually small cube-shaped crystals.

Properties of halite

Halite is clear or white when it comes out of the ground. Sometimes, halite crystals form with other minerals, giving it a tinted color. For example, if formed with clay, halite takes on a gray color. When placed under **ultraviolet light**, halite glows, or fluoresces, red, green, or orange. Halite is also soft, so it easily breaks into pieces.

Close up, these grains of salt from a salt shaker are cube-shaped.

Evaporites

Halite belongs to a group of minerals called evaporites. These minerals are **dissolved** in water. When water **evaporates**, the minerals are left behind as solids. Other minerals that are evaporites include gypsum and anhydrite, which are both used to make plaster and cement; borax, which is used to make detergent; and sulfur, used to make rubber and other products. These minerals are often found together in evaporite deposits.

Sodium and chlorine

Minerals are made up of different substances called **elements**. Halite is made up of the elements sodium and chlorine. Sodium is a bluish-white solid. Chlorine is a greenish-yellow **gas**. When joined together, they create the **compound** sodium chloride. Sodium chloride is the chemical name for salt.

Salt is an evaporite because it can be dissolved in water. People around the world harvest salt by evaporating water from the oceans.

This large sample of rock salt comes from a mine in Cheshire, England. It is yellowish-red because sand blew over it as it was forming millions of years ago.

Types of salts

Sodium chloride is called common salt. There are other types of minerals that are classified as salts, but do not have the same elements as sodium chloride. Examples of other salts are sylvite and epsomite. Sylvite is used as a substitute for table salt. It forms from the elements potassium and chlorine, and is found near volcanoes. Epsomite, or epsom salts, are used for healing. Epsomite is made up of the elements magnesium and sulfate, and forms in caves.

7

Salt water

There is salt in water in the world's oceans, in dried-up lakes in the deserts, and buried deep underground. All of the salt at one time was dissolved in salt water. Today, the world's main supply of salt is the oceans.

Not just water

Salt is made up of the elements sodium and chlorine. When sodium and chlorine are both present in water, they join together. Other elements are also found in water, such as magnesium, calcium, and potassium.

Ancient oceans

About four billion years ago, oceans began to form on Earth as ash, gases, and water vapor from volcanoes rose up to form clouds.

Scientists think that this may have caused constant rain for hundreds of years, until there was enough water to fill the oceans. The ancient oceans were not as salty as today's oceans.

(above) The areas around the North and South poles are the least salty parts of the oceans because frequent snow, rain, and melting ice dilute *the salt water.*

(below) Today, the water in the oceans contains three percent salt. There are about 1.2 ounces (34 grams) of salt dissolved in every quart (liter) of ocean water.

Why is water salty?

Chlorine is a volcanic gas, which means it is released when volcanoes erupt. It dissolves easily in water. Today, the ocean floor is littered with erupting volcanoes. As these volcanoes erupt, chlorine is dissolved into the water.

Sodium is an element that makes up **igneous rock**. When it rains, the **acidity** in water breaks down pieces of the rock, which get carried away by streams and rivers into oceans.

The rock cycle

Hot melted rock called magma lies beneath the Earth's outer rocky layer. When volcanoes erupt, the melted rock is spewed out as lava and later cools, forming a type of rock called igneous rock. Over time, weather erodes these rocks and breaks them down into pieces, called particles, and carries them away to the ocean. The particles settle on the ocean floor. As they pile up, a type of rock called sedimentary rock is formed. Sedimentary rock may eventually melt into the hot layer of Earth and erupt from volcanoes as lava again.

The process of erupting, cooling, and erupting again, is called the rock cycle.

(above) As water runs over rock, it breaks the rock down in a process called weathering.

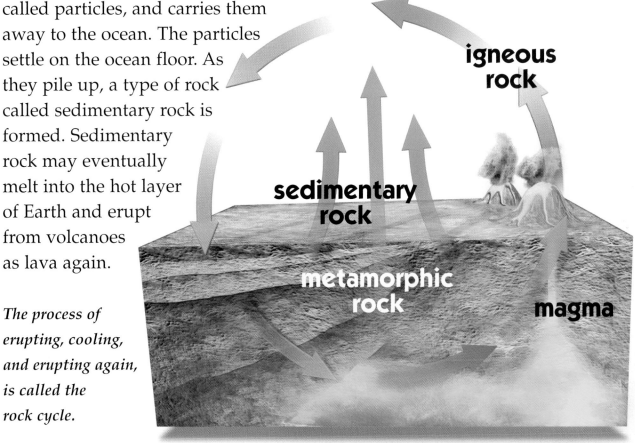

igneous rock

sedimentary rock

metamorphic rock

magma

Land of salt

Millions of years ago, saltwater oceans covered the continents. The Sun heated the water, and it began to evaporate. The sodium chloride that was dissolved in the water crystallized to form halite.

Salt flats

Playas are desert lakes that sometimes have salt flats. Salt flats are large tracts of land covered in salt where water has evaporated. Playas only last a short time because water evaporates quickly in the desert. The largest salt flat in the world is the Uyuni Salt Flat in Bolivia, a country in South America. The salt flat covers about 4,000 square miles (10,360 square kilometers).

(above) Lake Bonneville once covered western Utah, eastern Nevada, and southern Idaho. Today, the area is a large salt flat in the desert. The dry flat area is used to race cars.

(right) Great Salt Lake in Utah was once part of larger Lake Bonneville. Other lakes that have very high salt levels are the Salton Sea and Mono Lake in California.

Salt lakes

Some salt lakes still exist today. The Dead Sea, for example, is a large lake in the Middle East between Israel and Jordan. It is ten times saltier than the ocean. Water continuously runs into the Dead Sea from rivers, carrying sodium with it. The Dead Sea is located in an area where volcanic gas from the Earth's crust leaks, supplying chlorine to the water. There is no outlet for water to drain out of the Dead Sea. Instead, water evaporates at a high rate because of the area's warm climate.

(above) Along the shores of the Dead Sea, salt crystallizes in strange-looking pillars as the water evaporates.

precipitation falls

vapor rises

sun heats water

The water cycle

Water moves in a never-ending cycle called the water cycle, or hydrologic cycle. During the cycle, water falls from clouds to Earth in the form of rain and snow. The water runs into rivers and lakes, which empty into the oceans. When the Sun heats the water, it evaporates, or turns into a gas. This gas is called water vapor. Water vapor rises up into the **atmosphere** and forms clouds.

Bedded salt deposits

Salt is buried underground in areas of the world that do not have dry climates. If the salt were on the surface, it would dissolve in rainwater. The salt found in these parts of the world was once part of ancient oceans. The oceans evaporated, and over time, salt in these basins was buried under **sediment**. The sediment weighed down on the salt crystals, which pressed together to form hard rock. This underground rock is called bedded salt deposits. Today, the salt beds are from 500 to 7,000 feet (152 to 2,134 meters) below the surface and about 1000 to 3000 feet (305 to 9014 meters) thick. On top and below the salt beds are layers of sedimentary rock. Large areas of bedded salt are found in Cheshire in England, Stassfurt in Germany, Salzburg in Austria, and areas around the Great Lakes in North America.

(above) This chapel is located in a salt mine in Colombia. The walls are salt.

(below) Rock salt from a mine in the Sahara desert in Africa.

Salt domes

Salt domes are areas where salt that is less **dense** than the rock above it, flowed upward. There are two forms of salt domes. An "island" is a raised landform pushed up from the pressure of salt rising from below. A **subsided** area occurs when water moving over the dome dissolves the salt faster than the salt is rising, causing the surface to sink down.

Salt is impermeable, which means that material cannot pass through it. As the salt domes formed thousands of years ago, organic, or once-living, materials became trapped by the rising salt. The materials decomposed, or rotted, to form oil and natural gas. Oil and natural gas are valuable sources of energy.

(right) Areas around salt domes form traps that contain oil, such as in Iran, Texas, and north Germany.

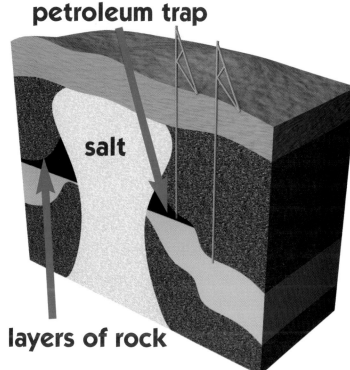

petroleum trap

salt

layers of rock

(above) Some salt domes are plug-shaped and also contain layers of potassium- and magnesium-rich salts.

Avery Island

Avery Island is one of five salt domes off the coast of Louisiana. The 2.5-square-mile (6.5-square-kilometer) island has been mined for salt since 1898. Today, 2.5 million tons (2.3 million tonnes) of salt from the island is shipped by barge up the Mississippi River each year to be used as road salt and in industry.

Salt mining

There are two ways to mine salt. One way is to dig it out of underground deposits. The other way is to pour liquid into the salt deposit, then allow the liquid to evaporate.

Room and pillar mining

In room and pillar mining, large bedded salt deposits and salt domes are mined by clearing areas of the deposit while leaving tall pillars, or columns, standing. These pillars support the ceiling of the mine, so it does not collapse. As much as 50 percent of the salt is left in the mines, so they do not collapse.

To get at bedded deposits of salt, a **shaft** is drilled down into the salt deposit. Equipment and miners are sent down the shaft.

Large machines called undercutters clear tunnels into the "room" to be mined. A drilling rig is used to drill holes into the salt. Explosives are placed in the holes, and the salt is blasted apart into large chunks. Front-end loaders then move the huge pieces of salt to a crusher, which is a machine that grinds salt into smaller pieces. The salt is then loaded on a conveyer belt and taken to the surface.

A miner stands by a conveyor belt carrying salt to a crusher in a mine. After the salt is crushed, it is packaged and sold.

The inside of this German salt mine was used to store planes during World War II.

Solution mining

Salt buried deeper beneath the surface is usually extracted by solution mining. In solution mining, hot water is pumped down into a salt deposit. The hot water dissolves the salt into a thick salty substance called brine. Brine is about thirty percent salt. The brine is pumped back up to the surface where it is sent through a pipeline to a purification plant. At the plant, other minerals, such as calcium and magnesium, that may be mixed in with the brine are removed. The remaining fluid is then evaporated.

Salt caverns

Salt caverns are large empty spaces left underground after the salt has been removed. These spaces are sometimes used to store oil and gas. Some companies want to use the hollow spaces to store **hazardous waste**.

Finding salt

Geologists are scientists who study the physical history of Earth, especially by studying rocks. To find salt domes, geologists send **seismic waves** into the ground. Using computers to monitor the way these waves travel through Earth's layers, they can guess what lies beneath the surface.

This geologist is reading electronic equipment from the inside of a truck used for sending waves into the ground.

15

Solar salt

Salt water is evaporated by heating it in salt pans. Salt pans, or ponds, are natural or human-made depressions in the ground. When dried by the sun and wind, the salt is called solar salt. Thirty percent of all salt produced is solar salt. Solar evaporation is the oldest method of producing salt.

Evaporation dams

Salt water is pumped into large evaporation dams, where it is evaporated by the sun. Other minerals in the water are left in the bottom of the pans. More salt water is added to the dams, so that as the water evaporates, the brine has more salt in it. When the brine holds as much salt as it can, it is pumped into reservoirs, or large holding areas.

(top) This woman in China is using hand tools to harvest salt. The piles of salt behind her have been raked from the bottom of crystallization pans.

(right) Canals are built between solar pans to drain water away from the salt.

Crystallization pans

From reservoirs, the brine is moved to crystallization pans, which are rectangle shaped and made from clay or concrete. The crystallization pans are connected by roadways and channels. Specially built canals are dug alongside the pans to drain rainwater, so that the brine does not become diluted. Water evaporates until salt crystallizes at the bottom of the pans. When all the salt has crystallized, the remaining fluid is drained.

This huge pile of salt was harvested from the ocean off the coast of New Zealand.

Harvesting salt

Harvesting starts when a large amount of salt has accumulated. Machines dig up the salt and dump it onto conveyer belts that take the salt to trucks. In some places, the salt is harvested by hand, using rakes and other hand-held tools. Once the salt had been gathered, it is washed in brine to remove dirt and allowed to dry out again.

Refining

After the salt has been dried, it is sterilized, which means all the remaining unwanted parts are taken out. The salt is then crushed and put onto screens. The screens are used to sort salt into its different sizes after it has been crushed. The salt is packaged by size - coarse, medium, or fine.

Salt from a harvester is loaded into rail cars to be taken to a refining plant.

Salt in history

At one time, people got the salt they needed by eating meat. The earliest record of salt production is from China, about 5,000 years ago.

Ancient Egyptians

In ancient Egypt, a form of salt called **natron** was used to mummify the bodies of kings and other rich and powerful people. Natron was found along the Nile River, in Egypt. It dried out the bodies, so they did not rot. Natron was also used to preserve fish, olives, cheese, and meat.

The Salineras de Maras are salt pans in the Sacred Valley of the Inca, in Peru. Salt has been harvested there since before the Spanish arrived in the 1500s.

Salt trade

Along the Mediterranean Sea, countries such as France, Spain, and Italy developed a route for trading salt. The Via Salaria, or Salt Road, was one of the first roads built by the **ancient Romans** and was used to bring salt to Rome from the coast. For over 2,000 years people in this dry warm climate have been producing solar salt. The dried salt was carried by mules over the mountains and traded with people from parts of northern Europe.

For several thousand years, these salt pans in Malta, an island in the Mediterranean, have been used to evaporate salt water.

The Middle Ages

The Middle Ages in Europe lasted from about 500 A.D. to 1500 A.D. During this time, salt was used as a preservative for meat, fish, and vegetables. Crops were harvested in the late autumn, and because of the cold climate in most of Europe, fresh food could not be grown until the next spring. Salting food was one of the only ways of making sure that people had enough food to last the winter. Salt was valuable, but it was also hard to get, as people did not yet have the tools to mine it. Peasants, or poor farmers, often had to pay high taxes for salt, or eat their meat rotten. In some countries, peasants revolted over the salt taxes.

(above) In this illustration from the Middle Ages, salt is being evaporated over an oven.

Native Americans

In North America, Native Americans were using salt long before contact with Europeans. For example, the Zuni Pueblo Native Peoples of present-day New Mexico used salt to make bread and to boil dumplings. They carried salt on their journeys and would celebrate when men from the tribe returned from a salt-gathering expedition.

Exploring the New World

European fishers first explored the coasts of North America in the 1400s, looking for cod. To preserve the fish to take it back to Europe, it was rubbed with salt. Eventually, French and British fishers learned a preserving method called dry salting. To dry salt the fish, the fishers hung the salted fish over racks on the shore. They started to build houses and small villages on the east coast of North America. These small villages led to permanent settlements.

In this illustration, European fishers are dry salting cod.

Chemical industry

Starting in the 1700s, great progress was made in chemistry in Europe. Scientists were discovering how to extract sodium and chlorine from salt to make soap and other products. As a result, demand for salt increased and people started to look for other ways of getting the mineral. At the same time, drilling techniques were also improving. Bedded salt deposits were being located and mined.

Salt and war

During the **American Revolution**, the British tried to create a salt shortage by stopping ships carrying the cargo. This prompted the **colonists** to develop more sources of salt in North America. At first, they tried boiling ocean water in their homes but found they could not produce enough salt to meet their needs. Along the east coast of North America, saltworks were established. The North American salt industry continued to grow until it became the biggest in the world.

Today, an international organization called the Salt Institute works to find more ways to use salt, and to provide information and research into the history and future of salt use.

Religion and salt

Salt also plays a role in some religious practices. For Jewish people, salt is used to make meat kosher by removing the blood from it. According to the Torah, or Jewish holy book, meat must be slaughtered and prepared in a specific way.

The oldest working salt mine in Europe is in Krakow, Poland. The Wieliczka mine has been operating for over 700 years. The first miners here were prisoners of war, who worked the mines under slave-like conditions until their deaths. By the 1500s, the mines had become so deep that pulleys and horses were used to hoist the salt to the surface.

The salt producers

Every country in the world has access to salt, either along its shores or beneath Earth's surface. The way a country produces salt depends on its climate. Most countries produce enough salt to meet their needs, with the exception of Japan, which imports salt from Australia.

North America

In the United States and Canada, most salt is mined from underground because the climate in most places is not warm or dry enough to evaporate salt from ocean water. Large beds of rock salt are located south of the Great Lakes, under southern Ontario, Michigan, Ohio, Pennsylvania, New York, and West Virginia.

Bedded salt deposits are also mined in Texas and Louisiana. The United States is the largest producer and consumer of salt.

Europe

Similar to North America, northern European countries are too cold and wet to produce salt by evaporation. In countries such as Germany, Poland, Russia, and England, salt is mined from underground. In southern European countries where it is warmer and there is a source of seawater, such as France, Italy, and Spain, salt is produced by both mining and solar evaporation.

In California, salt can be produced by solar evaporation because of the warm climate.

India is one of the world's largest producers of salt.

Asia

China was probably the first place in the world where solution mining took place. Today, China has a lot of underground salt, but most of China's salt production is through solar evaporation of seawater and inland salt lakes. In India and islands in the Pacific Ocean, most salt is produced through solar evaporation.

Island salt

Starting in the 1600s, the islands in the Caribbean Sea were used for solar evaporation of salt. The Dutch and English established colonies on the islands. Slaves were sent to rake and harvest the salt, and European ships carried it to North American colonies where it was used to preserve food. Today, on Great Inagua Island in the Bahamas, and Bonaire, an island in the south Caribbean, North American companies still use local labor to produce salt for export.

The salt industry on the Caribbean islands was built on slave labor. For a few hours a night, the slaves slept in huts, such as these, on Bonaire.

Uses of salt

There are three main uses of salt - to flavor food, to preserve food, and to keep the roads clear of snow and ice. Sodium and chlorine are taken out of salt and used in the chemical industry to make a whole range of other useful products.

Pass the salt, please!

Solar salt is also called sea salt and is used in cooking. Solution-mined salt can also be refined and used as common table salt. From salt, other seasonings are made. For example, garlic salt is salt mixed with ground garlic. Hickory salt is salt mixed with ground hickory wood. It gives food a smokey flavor.

Before there was refrigeration to keep food from going bad, food was salted. Salting is still used today to prevent cheese, pickles, sauerkraut, nuts, and even potato chips from going bad.

Salt absorbs moisture from food, preventing bacteria and other germs from making food go bad.

To salt meat, it is rubbed with salt and placed in a salting tub, which is a large container usually made of clay. The pieces of meat are left in the tub for about 60 days. Salted meat is usually boiled in water to remove some of the salt before it is eaten.

There are a variety of different salts used as seasonings for food.

(left) During the international conflict called World War I (1914-1918), mustard gas was used to kill enemy soldiers in trenches. Mustard gas burns the skin and lungs. It was made from the gas chlorine.

Road salt

Over half of all the salt produced in North America is used on icy roads. Most of this salt comes from underground mined salt. Salt freezes at 28.6 degrees Fahrenheit (-1.9 degrees Celsius), and water freezes at 32 degrees Fahrenheit (0 degrees Celsius). When rock salt is put on ice-covered roads, the area around the salt begins to melt because the **freezing point** has been lowered.

(below) Large trucks transport rock salt to be used on icy roads. The rock salt is sometimes mixed with sand.

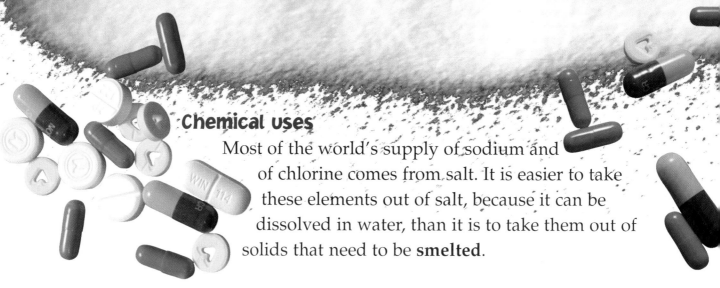

Chemical uses

Most of the world's supply of sodium and of chlorine comes from salt. It is easier to take these elements out of salt, because it can be dissolved in water, than it is to take them out of solids that need to be **smelted**.

Sodium

The most popular use of sodium is to combine it with hydroxide to make sodium hydroxide, also known as caustic soda. On its own, caustic soda is a dangerous chemical that burns human skin. It is so powerful that it is used in homes to unclog drains by burning its way through muck. In industry, caustic soda is used to make paper, cellophane, and a cloth called rayon.

Probably one of the most useful products around the home is made from sodium - sodium bicarbonate, or baking soda. This white powder was first discovered by a Belgian chemist named Ernest Solvay (1838-1922) in the 1860s. Since then, baking soda has been used as an ingredient in baking to make baked goods rise, help relieve heartburn, whiten teeth, and absorb odors.

Chlorine

The most popular use of chlorine is as a **disinfectant**. Chlorine kills germs and bacteria and is used to keep swimming pools clean, and to make bleach and drugs. Most chlorine is used as an ingredient in paint, plastic, and **pesticides**.

At this processing plant, chlorine is separated from seawater by electrolysis.

(below) Caustic soda is a product of sodium used in the pulp and paper industry.

Electrolysis

Sodium and chlorine are extracted from salt by a process called electrolysis. Electrolysis was discovered by British chemist Sir Humphry Davy (1778-1829) in 1807. To extract the elements from salt, it is first dissolved in water. An **electrical current** is then passed through the water, breaking the **bonds** that hold the elements together.

Salt and the body

The human body contains salt. The body cannot make its own salt - it comes from the food we eat.

Beep beep

The body is made up of **cells**, which are surrounded by fluids. Sodium from the salt we eat is essential for many of the body's functions. When we move, it is because a signal has been sent from our brains to our muscles. In order for this signal to be sent, sodium enters our cells from the surrounding fluid, where it reacts with potassium, creating the signal.

(right) Blood is pumped around our bodies through veins and arteries.

(below) Extra salt from our bodies is lost when we are active and we sweat.

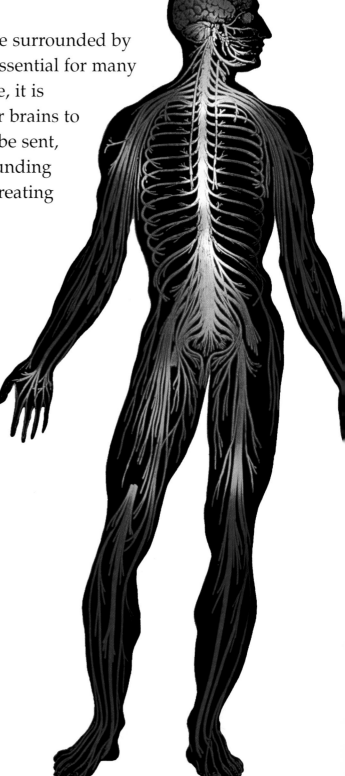

Bodily fluids

Many of our bodily fluids contain salt. We **excrete** excess salt in our urine and tears. In our stomachs, food is broken down into the nutrients our bodies need. In the stomach, a fluid called hydrochloric acid, which contains a form of chlorine, helps digest the food.

High blood pressure

Blood is pumped around the body through tubes called arteries and blood vessels. The heart is the muscle that does the pumping. The pressure of blood pushing against the blood vessels is called blood pressure. Salt in the blood attracts fluid from cells in the body. More fluid in the blood makes the heart work harder and causes blood pressure to go up. This strain can cause heart attacks. One way to reduce the risk of high blood pressure is to eat a diet low in salt.

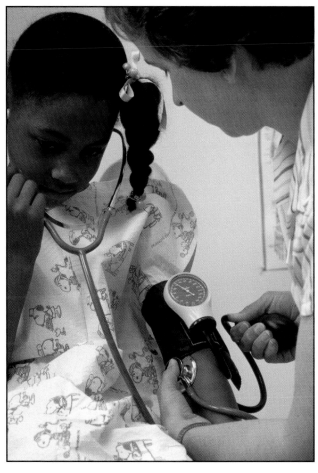

(above) This girl is having her blood pressure checked. In most cases, high blood pressure is a condition that older adults get.

(right) There is about 5.5 ounces (155 grams) of salt in the human body. Most of this salt is present without adding extra salt to food.

Salt and nature

Animals and plants living in the oceans and salt marshes, which are areas of low wetland often covered by saltwater tides, have adapted ways of getting or extracting salt. Salt pollution occurs in areas where humans have introduced salt into fresh water.

Salt and animals

Animals are attracted to salt because their bodies need it to stay healthy. Animals in forests find salt on their own. On farms, salt licks are put out for animals, such as cows and horses. Salt licks are bricks of salt that also contain other minerals to keep animals healthy.

Animals that live in salt marshes and oceans have ways of getting rid of excess salt. For example, flamingos mostly live in salt marshes and lakes. They have adapted to these environments by being able to drink hot water from nearby **geysers** and by having specialized **glands** near their eyes that make salty water. The salty liquid leaves their bodies through their nostrils.

Salt pollution

The rock salt spread onto icy roads can seep through the soil and into underground water supplies, eventually ending up in freshwater lakes. Large quantities of salt pollute the water, which can harm the animals living there, and drain the nutrients from the soil in the area.

Salt pollution is also caused by food-processing plants. The salty brine used to preserve food, as well as the waste water containing chlorine for disinfecting, has to be disposed of. Governments around the world and environmental groups have made it necessary for these plants to clean the water first, before disposing of it.

This deer in Waterton National Park, in Alberta, Canada, has quenched its desire for salt by licking road salt from car tires.

If rock salt for de-icing roads is not properly stored, it can cause salt pollution by leaking into the water supply.

Desalination plants

At desalination plants, salt is taken out from seawater, making the water fresh enough for people to drink. Desalination is most commonly done through a process called distillation. To distill salt water, it is heated into a vapor, then very quickly **condensed** again before the minerals in it have a chance to dissolve back into the water. The first distillation plant was on Curacao, an island in the Caribbean Sea, in 1928. Since then, desalination plants have been established all over the world.

Glossary

acidity An acid or sour quality

American Revolution A war between the American colonies and Great Britain (1775 to 1783), at the end of which America gained its independence

ancient Romans People of a empire lasting from 27 B.C. to 410 A.D. and extending from Egypt to England at its most powerful

atmosphere The layers of gases surrounding Earth

atoms The smallest unit of an element. Atoms cannot be seen without a microscope

bonds The forces, or attractions, between two elements that hold them together

cells The smallest and most basic parts of plants and animals

chemical A substance produced by chemistry

colonists People who settled in faraway lands but remained citizens of their home country

compound A substance formed from joining two or more elements

condensed Changed from a gas to a liquid

dense Having parts tightly packed together

dilute To reduce the strength of a liquid by adding water

disinfectant A chemical substance made to destroy germs

dissolved Mixed thoroughly with a liquid

electrical current An ordered movement of electrically charged particles

elements A group of 100 substances that each has its own kind of atoms

evaporated Changed from a liquid to a gas

excrete To get rid of waste matter

freezing point The temperature a liquid freezes at

gas Neither solid nor liquid

geysers Crevices in the ground through which steam and hot water escape

glands Specialized cells that produce substances that the body gives off

igneous rock Rock formed from hardened lava

hazardous waste Waste that is harmful to the environment

natron A type of salt used in mummification

pesticides Chemicals used to kill small pests

sediment Sand and stones deposited by water or wind

seismic waves Natural or human-caused vibrations of the Earth

shaft A long narrow vertical passage

smelted Melted a solid to extract its parts

subsided Sink down

three-dimensional Appearing to have length, width, and depth

ultraviolet light Rays, or beams, of energy

Index

1 2 3 4 5 6 7 8 9 0 Printed in the USA 0 9 8 7 6 5 4 3 2 1